The Little Black Book on
Social Security
Maximization

Retirement Lifestyle Advocates

The Little Black Book on
Social Security Maximization

Copyright © 2019 Retirement Lifestyle Advocates

Published in the United States of America

By PLP Services, LLC
Grand Rapids, Michigan

This publication is designed to provide accurate and authoritative information in regard to the subject matter covered. It is offered with the understanding that the publisher is not engaged in rendering legal, accounting, or other professional services. If legal advice or other expert assistance is required, the services of a competent professional person should be sought.

To order your Social Security maximization analysis, simply visit
www.SocialSecurityMaximizationReport.com

Table of Contents

To order your Social Security
maximization analysis, simply visit
www.SocialSecurityMaximizationReport.com

CHAPTER ONE

Social Security: The Perfect Political Scheme at the Perfect Time

President Franklin Roosevelt signing the Social Security Act on August 14, 1935

I don't mean to be glib by using the word "scheme" to describe the origination and implementation of Social Security benefits.

But when you take a look at when and how Social Security began, it seems like the best word to use.

The Social Security Act became law on August 14, 1935, when President Franklin Roosevelt signed the bill.

As one might expect from a politician, Mr. Roosevelt had some predictably eloquent remarks for the occasion.

> *Young people have come to wonder what would be their lot when they came to old age. The man with a job has wondered how long the job would last.*

> *This social security measure gives at least some protection to thirty millions of our citizens who will reap direct benefits through unemployment compensation, through old-age pensions and through increased services for the protection of children and the prevention of ill health.*

> *We can never insure one hundred percent of the population against one hundred percent of the hazards and vicissitudes of life, but we have tried to frame a law which will give some measure of protection to the average citizen and to his family against the loss of a job and against poverty-ridden old age.*

> *This law, too, represents a cornerstone in a structure which is being built but is*

by no means complete. It is a structure intended to lessen the force of possible future depressions. It will act as a protection to future Administrations against the necessity of going deeply into debt to furnish relief to the needy. The law will flatten out the peaks and valleys of deflation and of inflation. It is, in short, a law that will take care of human needs and at the same time provide the United States an economic structure of vastly greater soundness.

Despite Roosevelt's assuring articulateness, Social Security, at the time, provided a government safety net to only a small segment of the population.

One of the original Social Security promotional pamphlets

But the first rule of politics is never to let the facts get in the way of sounding knowledgeable and compassionate.

The reality of the Social Security program in 1935 was that it was the perfect political proposal. The normal retirement age for someone who wanted to participate in Social Security, this new government-sponsored pension program, and receive full retirement benefits was age 65.[1] Yet the average life expectancy for an American at the time was 61 years.[2]

You can just see the politicians of the day in the proverbial smoke-filled room rubbing their hands together and slapping each other on the back as they contrived this program that would provide a current benefit to only a minority of Americans.

It was perfectly designed: a political victory as well as a tax revenue victory!

Social Security, at least in the beginning, was a cash cow for the tax coffers of the Washington politicians. There were 37 workers paying Social Security taxes in 1935 for every 1 worker collecting benefits.[3]

As long as the average American continued to die before becoming eligible for full retirement, what could go wrong?

Initially, beginning in 1937, workers and employers each paid 1% of the worker's annual wages, up to $3,000 in Social Security taxes. One of the initial publications explaining to the public how the Social Security program would work proclaimed that the 1% tax rate was "the most you will ever pay."

That brings us to the second rule of politics: always retain the option of changing your mind if it's in the "national interest" or for the "social good."

That's what happened in the case of Social Security. While the initial employee and employer tax rate of 1% remained static through the calendar year 1949, by 1950 the Social Security or FICA, tax rate increased by 50% to 1.5%.[4]

Over time, as usually happens with taxes, the Social Security tax rate increased, as did the wage base on which the tax was calculated.

The demographics surrounding Social Security changed, and changed dramatically. And, as usually happens with government programs, Social Security was expanded, adding disability benefits in 1956 and an automatic cost-of-living adjustment in 1975.[5]

As the Social Security program expanded, so did program costs. Further, as demographics changed, and people started living longer, program costs increased as well.

According to some sources, average life expectancy in the United States for both men and woman has increased two years per decade since the 1950s. That means that in the last 60

Employee Social

Year(s)	Security Tax Rate	Wage Base
1937–1949	1.0%	$ 3,000
1950	1.5%	$ 3,000
1951–1953	1.5%	$ 3,600
1954	2.0%	$ 3,600
1955–1956	2.0%	$ 4,200
1957–1958	2.25%	$ 4,200
1959	2.50%	$ 4,800
1960–1961	3.0%	$ 4,800
1962	3.125%	$ 4,800
1963–1965	3.625%	$ 4,800
1966	3.85%	$ 6,600
1967	3.9%	$ 6,600
1968	3.8%	$ 7,800
1969–1970	4.2%	$ 7,800
1971	4.6%	$ 7,800
1972	4.6%	$ 9,000
1973	4.85%	$ 10,800
1974	4.95%	$ 13,200
1975	4.95%	$ 14,100
1976	4.95%	$ 15,200
1977	4.95%	$ 16,500
1978	5.05%	$ 17,700
1979	5.08%	$ 22,900
1980	5.08%	$ 25,900
1981	5.35%	$ 29,700
1982	5.4%	$ 32,400
1983	5.4%	$ 35,700
1984	5.7%	$ 37,800
1985	5.7%	$ 39,600
1986	5.7%	$ 42,000
1987	5.7%	$ 43,800

Employee Social

Year(s)	Security Tax Rate	Wage Base
1988	6.06%	$ 45,000
1989	6.06%	$ 48,000
1990	6.2%	$ 51,300
1991	6.2%	$ 53,400
1992	6.2%	$ 55,500
1993	6.2%	$ 57,600
1994	6.2%	$ 60,600
1995	6.2%	$ 61,200
1996	6.2%	$ 62,700
1997	6.2%	$ 65,400
1998	6.2%	$ 68,400
1999	6.2%	$ 72,600
2000	6.2%	$ 76,200
2001	6.2%	$ 80,400
2002	6.2%	$ 84,900
2003	6.2%	$ 87,000
2004	6.2%	$ 87,900
2005	6.2%	$ 90,000
2006	6.2%	$ 94,200
2007	6.2%	$ 97,500
2008	6.2%	$102,000
2009	6.2%	$106,800
2010	6.2%	$106,800
2011	6.2%	$106,800
2012	6.2%	$110,100
2013	6.2%	$113,700
2014	6.2%	$117,000
2015	6.2%	$117,000
2016	6.2%	$118,500
2017	6.2%	$127,200
2018	6.2%	$128,400

years, the average American collects 144 more Social Security checks than their grandparents or great-grandparents.

What is not illustrated on the previous chart are the additional taxes paid for Medicare. While Medicare taxes used to be subject to an earnings cap like Social Security taxes, that has changed. Presently, all earnings are subject to Medicare taxes.

As the chart clearly shows, as time has passed, Social Security tax rates have increased, as has the wage base on which Social Security taxes are paid. At the inception of the Social Security program, total employer and employee taxes could have been as high as $600 per year. In 2018, the employee and employer tax could amount to as much as $15,921. That's an increase of more than 2,650%.

By contrast, when comparing the purchasing power of a 1937 US dollar to the purchasing power of a 2018 dollar using the inflation calculator at the Bureau of Labor Statistics, you discover that it takes $17.90 in 2018 to buy what $1 bought in 1937. That's an increase of about 1,790%, far less than Social Security taxes have increased on a percentage basis.

Now, as also often happens with government programs, Social Security is significantly under-funded. According to the Social Security trust-ee's report,[6] it would take an additional $17.5 trillion to bring the Social Security program back into full solvency and pay all current and future Social Security benefits.

If you've looked closely at your Social Se-curity earnings statement lately, you know that according to Social Security's own calculations only 76% of promised benefits can be paid with the current level of funding.

And there's the issue of the Social Security trust fund, which, according to Social Security, has assets of about $2.5 trillion, but the reality is, that's just an accounting gimmick.

Here's some proof.

Back in 2011, when asked by a reporter if Social Security checks would go out if the gov-ernment was shut down, then President Barack Obama said this:

> I cannot guarantee that those checks go out on August 3rd if we haven't re-solved this issue. Because there may simply not be the money in the coffers to do it. [7]

How could that be?

Especially if there is a trust fund of $2.8 trillion. When one visits the Social Security Administration's website and peruses the trust fund data, there, in black and white, it says that there is a trust fund balance of more than $2.8 trillion.[8]

So again the pregnant question is: Why would Social Security checks not go out even if the squabbling Washington politicians can't agree on raising the federal debt limit?

The late, syndicated columnist Charles Krauthammer wrote this after Obama's Treasury Secretary, Jack Lew, stated that the Social Security trust fund had enough assets to pay benefits for 26 years:

> *This claim is a breathtaking fraud. The pretense is that a flush trust fund will pay retirees for the next 26 years. Lovely, except for one thing: The Social Security trust fund is a fiction. . . . In other words, the Social Security trust fund contains— nothing.[9]*

Here is how the Social Security trust fund works.

Perform this exercise.

Go get your checkbook and write yourself a check for $1 trillion. Now declare yourself the world's first trillionaire.

Now you get it. The trust fund is a paper asset with nothing to back it, just like your worthless trillion dollar check.

Moving ahead, there will have to be changes to the Social Security program. It's likely that the millennials will have a normal retirement age that is much older than the normal retirement ages of today. For some Social Security program recipients, the cost-of-living adjustment may be means tested, and for others a greater portion of their Social Security benefits may be subject to income tax.

That's why it's absolutely vital that you maximize your benefits from the Social Security program. And that's what this book is all about.

CHAPTER TWO

Social Security: How Your Benefit Is Calculated

The calculation to determine the level of Social Security benefits that you will receive is complex. While it's possible to manually calculate the benefit that you will ultimately receive from Social Security, it's far easier to use a reliable software program to calculate and model your different, potential Social Security collection methodologies. In Chapter Six, we will introduce you to one such program that is available at a very low cost.

However, it's important to point out that relying only on a software program to determine the best way for you to collect Social Security benefits can be dangerous. While a software program can make recommendations based on certain assumptions, what a software program cannot do is take into account all of your personal facts and circumstances. While using a reliable and accurate software program to help you maximize your Social Security benefits is essential, the software program recommendations should be considered in the context of your complete personal financial situation. Again, more on this in Chapter Six.

In this chapter, we will acquaint you with the Social Security benefit calculation, so you have a solid understanding of it. This understanding is necessary to determine the best way for you, or you and your spouse if you're married, to collect Social Security benefits.

To qualify for Social Security, 40 "credits" are required. A worker paying Social Security taxes can earn 4 credits per year, or 1 credit per quarter. Some quick math will reveal to you that 10 years of work is required at a minimum to qualify for benefits.

In the calendar year 2018, one needs to have a minimum of $1,329 in quarterly earnings to earn credit for that quarter. That translates to $5,280 in annual earnings at a minimum to qualify for 4 credits for the year.

Once a worker reaches 40 credits, that worker is fully insured for Social Security and qualifies for benefits.

When a worker becomes fully insured, the ultimate benefits received by that worker from

Social Security are determined by a formula that looks at the highest 35 years of earned income of which Social Security taxes, otherwise known as FICA taxes, are paid. (Note: FICA taxes are used to fund both Social Security and Medicare.)

If a worker hasn't worked for at least 35 years in a covered job, the years with no earnings will be counted as zero in the formula since there were no FICA taxes paid in those years.

On the other hand, if someone has worked at least 35 years or more in a covered job, then the highest 35 earnings years are used when calculating the worker's ultimate Social Security benefit.

This formula to determine the ultimate benefits from Social Security is the AIME formula, an acronym for Average Indexed Monthly Earnings.

As we discussed in Chapter One, the maximum income on which Social Security taxes are paid each year has risen over time, adjusting for inflation or the devaluation of the US dollar. In much the same way, the Average Indexed Monthly Earnings formula is also adjusted for inflation.

Here's an example to hopefully make the point clear. If you go back and look at the chart in Chapter One, you'll see that the maximum income on which Social Security taxes were paid in 1973 was $10,800. In the calendar year 2018, the maximum income on which Social Security taxes are paid is $128,700. The AIME formula adjusts earlier years for inflation. For example, the $10,800 earnings maximum from 1973 would be adjusted today to about $55,000. Earnings after age 60 are not indexed.

This inflation adjustment takes place for all earnings years, and then the best 35 years are selected when calculating the Social Security benefit to which a worker is entitled. The inflation-adjusted earnings of all 35 years are added together and then divided by 420 (35 years x 12 months each year). That provides you with your AIME number, or Average Indexed Monthly Earnings.

It is that number that is used to calculate your Primary Insurance Amount (PIA) under Social Security. The Primary Insurance Amount is the benefit amount that you will begin to collect at your Normal Retirement Age.

In the calendar year 2016, the highest possible AIME was $9,341. Here is how the PIA is calculated from the AIME.

The first $856 of AIME gets multiplied by 90%. $856 times 90% = $770.

The next $4,301 of AIME gets multiplied by 32%. $4,301 times 32% = $1,377.

The last $4,274 of AIME gets multiplied by 15%. $4,274 times 15% = $641.

That means the maximum Primary Insurance Amount is calculated as follows: $770 + $1,377 + $641 = $2,788.

As you probably already noticed, the first dollars of AIME are more heavily weighted when determining the PIA; that is to replace more income for lower-earning Social Security program participants.

The PIA is the benefit that you receive from Social Security at your Normal Retirement Age.

If you draw Social Security benefits at an age younger than your Normal Retirement Age, your Primary Insurance Amount is discounted and, if you defer, or delay collecting benefits from Social Security until after your Normal Retirement Age, your Social Security benefits will increase.

More detail on Social Security collection options in the next chapter.

SOCIAL SECURITY MAXIMIZATION

CHAPTER THREE

Social Security: Basic Collection Options

In this chapter, we'll examine different Social Security collection options. Most all Social Security collection options are based on two factors, your Primary Insurance Amount and your Normal Retirement Age. Both of these terms were defined in the last chapter.

Your Normal Retirement Age will vary based on your birth year.

Birth Year	Normal Retirement Age
1943–1954	66
1955	66 and 2 months
1956	66 and 4 months
1957	66 and 6 months
1958	66 and 8 months
1959	66 and 10 months

At your Normal Retirement Age, you will be eligible to collect your Primary Insurance Amount as determined by the Average Indexed Monthly

Earnings formula in the last chapter.

You can, however, elect to collect your Social Security benefits prior to your Normal Retirement Age. Unless you're disabled, the earliest age at which you can collect Social Security benefits is 62.

Should you make the decision to collect Social Security benefits at age 62, the benefit that you collect will be your Primary Insurance Amount discounted by a percentage. The percentage by which your Primary Insurance Amount is discounted will depend on your Normal Retirement Age as noted by the chart below.

Normal Retirement Age	Discount at 62
66	25%
66 and 2 months	25.83%
66 and 4 months	26.67%
66 and 6 months	27.50%
66 and 8 months	28.33%
66 and 10 months	29.17%
67	30%

For example, if your Primary Insurance Amount is $2,000 per month and your Normal Retirement Age is 66, should you opt to collect

Social Security benefits at age 62, your Primary Insurance Amount of $2,000 monthly will be discounted by 25%, or $500.

Your choice is to draw $1,500 per month at age 62, or wait and draw $2,000 monthly at your Normal Retirement Age of 66.

What's the best move here?

It depends.

It depends on your own, personal facts and circumstances. If you're still working and earning a good amount of money, it probably makes sense to wait until your Normal Retirement Age to collect Social Security benefits since there is an earnings limit that could adversely affect the Social Security benefits that you collect prior to your Normal Retirement Age.

In 2018, if you are collecting Social Security benefits and you have not yet reached your Normal Retirement Age, if you earn more than $17,040 in wages, for every $2 you earn over that threshold, you will give up $1 of Social Security benefits.

Let's assume you're 62 and still working and you earn $40,000 in a year. You want to decide if it makes sense to collect Social Security benefits now, at age 62, or if it makes more sense to wait and collect later, perhaps at your Normal Retirement Age. If you elect to collect Social Security benefits now, you'd collect $1,500 per month or $18,000 per year in Social Security benefits. If you're also earning $40,000 per year, you would give up some of your Social Security benefits. Here is the math:

$40,000 earnings – $17,040 earnings limit = $22,960.

$22,960 / 2 = $11,480 in Social Security benefits withheld.

In this example, Social Security would withhold ALL benefit payments beginning in January until the forfeited amount is paid, then regular benefit payments would continue for the rest of the year.

At the beginning of each year, Social Security will request that you estimate your income. The withholding for the year will then be based on that estimate. Any discrepancies will be made up in January of the following year after your income has been reported to the IRS.

In the calendar year in which you reach your Normal Retirement Age, the earnings test changes and becomes more lenient. If your Normal Retirement Age is 66 in 2018, you can earn up to $45,360 in the months before your birthday and not lose any benefits.

If you earn more than $45,360, you would give up $1 for every $3 in earnings that you have over $45,360.

If you draw Social Security benefits at age 62 and you retire at age 62, earnings prior to your retirement date do not adversely affect your Social Security benefits. Here's an example to make the point clear. A worker turns age 62 on October 30 and retires on her birthday. Prior to retirement on that date, she has earned $50,000. Now, after retirement, the earnings limit applies since she is younger than her Normal Retirement Age; however, the annual earnings limit of $17,040 is prorated monthly to $1,420 ($17,040/12 = $1,420). During her first two months of retirement, during the months of November and December, the earnings limit calculation would take place on a monthly basis.

It's important to understand that we're talking about earnings from a job or net self-employment income here. Passive income like income from investments or retirement accounts is not included in the formula.

The benefits that are withheld by Social Security while you continue to work are not lost forever. Once you reach your Normal Retirement Age, your monthly benefit will be increased to account for all the months in which benefits were withheld. For example, if you claimed benefits at age 62 but gave up 24 months of benefits over the next four years due to the earnings test, Social Security would adjust your benefit at full retirement age as if you had first claimed at age 64 not age 62, which would give you a higher benefit moving forward.

The earnings test no longer applies when you have attained your Normal Retirement Age.

It's also worth noting here that if a spouse or dependent is drawing Social Security benefits based on your earnings record, those benefits are also withheld while the earnings test is satisfied.

In many cases, if you intend to continue to work and earn a good income, it probably makes sense to consider waiting to collect your Social Security benefits until your Normal Retirement Age at a minimum.

If you are not planning on working and earning more than the earnings limit, the question is, should you draw Social Security benefits at age 62 or wait until age 66?

When trying to make this decision, many aspiring Social Security program recipients use the term "break-even point." While it is not a technical Social Security term, it's one that practically everyone uses.

Let's calculate the break-even point for Social Security benefits when first collecting benefits at age 62 versus age 66.

In the previous example, the age 62 benefit from Social Security is $1,500 per month or $18,000 annually. By drawing Social Security at age 62, one will collect $72,000 by age 66. We'll call that a "head start" amount.

At age 66, the benefit paid by Social Security will be $2,000 monthly or $24,000 per year, or $6,000 more than could be collected at age 62.

The math is straightforward. The head start amount of $72,000 is divided by the additional, annual benefit of $6,000; that gives us a "break-even" point of 12 years, or age 78 in this example.

Of course, that break-even point is not indexed for inflation. To be fair when making this calculation, we'd have to assume that a dollar in the future will buy less than a dollar does today. Depending on what inflation factor you want to use, the break-even point may be further out than age 78 given a dollar collected today from Social Security will probably buy more than a dollar collected at a future point. The reality is the real break-even point is a bit further out than age 78 in terms of real dollars.

When collecting Social Security, there is also the option of reaching your Normal Retirement Age and then waiting to collect benefits. When you make this decision, the final benefit that you collect from Social Security increases at a rate of .67% per month, or 8% per year.

In the example above, assuming a Normal Retirement Age of 66 and a Primary Insurance Amount of $2,000 monthly, for each month that Social Security benefits are deferred, the benefit increases $13.40; if Social Security benefits are deferred for one year, the monthly benefit reaches $2,160.

Social Security benefits can be deferred or delayed until age 70. There is no financial benefit to deferring benefits past age 70. Again, assuming a Normal Retirement Age of 66 and a Primary Insurance Amount of $2,000 monthly, the Primary Insurance Amount increases by a factor of 32% (8% per year x 4 years) to get the ultimate monthly benefit amount to $2,640 at age 70.

On an annual basis in this example, the Social Security benefit collected at age 66 is $24,000 annually; at age 70 it's $31,680 per year.

Let's walk through the break-even calculation again. Drawing Social Security benefits at one's Normal Retirement Age of 66 would mean that by age 70, there was a head start amount collected of $96,000. However, at age 70 the additional annual benefit collected from Social Security will be $7,680 per year. Again, the math is straightforward: the head start amount of $96,000 is divided by the additional, annual benefit of $7,680 to determine the break-even point ($96,000 head start/$7,680 additional annual benefit = 12.5-year break-even point).

In this case, drawing Social Security benefits at age 70 versus age 66 has a break-even point of age 82½ without considering an adjustment for inflation.

Then, assuming earned income is not an issue, there is the comparison of drawing Social Security benefits at age 62 versus age 70.

In this example, annual benefits at age 62 are $18,000, while benefits at age 70 are $31,680 per year. Electing to draw Social Security benefits at age 62 has one drawing total benefits of $144,000—that's the head start amount. At age 70, the additional benefit received per year is $13,680. Once again, we take the head start amount and divide by the additional annual benefit to determine the break-even point ($144,000 head start/$13,680 additional income = 10.52 years).

The non-inflation-adjusted break-even for drawing Social Security benefits at age 62 versus 70 is about age 80½.

All of these calculations and outcomes are driven significantly by individual facts and circumstances. When modeling different calculation methodologies, it's helpful to have a software system to quickly make the calculations and draw the logical comparisons.

More on software and income modeling to help you determine the best time for you to draw Social Security benefits in Chapter Six.

CHAPTER FOUR

Social Security Taxation: Reducing the Social Security Benefits of Many Americans

As we discussed in Chapter One, there are many problems facing the Social Security program currently. Demographics have dramatically changed since the inception of the Social Security program. Life expectancies have markedly increased, throwing the original actuarial assumptions of the Social Security program way out of whack.

According to some sources, the average life expectancy of both males and females in the United States has increased two years every decade since 1950. That means the life expectancy of an average American has increased 12 years in that relatively short time frame.

This demographic shift, combined with the fact that the Social Security trust fund has no real assets, has made Social Security a hand-to-mouth program. In 2010, the Social Security program began to collect less in taxes than it paid out in benefits.[10]

The solvency of the Social Security program is something that has been a frequent topic of conversation historically.

Back in the early 1980s, newly elected President Ronald Reagan appointed a committee to research and recommend solvency solutions for Social Security. That committee, which became known as the Greenspan Commission after the committee's chair, Alan Greenspan, made two recommendations that were eventually implemented. The first was to raise the Normal Retirement Age from 65 to 67 over a long period of time.

The second was to make Social Security benefits taxable for affluent and some upper-middle-income taxpayers. Beginning in 1983, up to 50% of Social Security benefits were included as income on the tax return of some taxpayers.

Later, in 1993, up to 85% of Social Security benefits could be taxable for some taxpayers.[11]

The original formula, implemented in 1983, to determine how much of one's Social Security would be taxable was known as the Modified Adjusted Gross Income (MAGI) formula.

The formula, predictably, was not simple, as it was developed in Washington.

Here's how MAGI was calculated in 1983:

½ Social Security Income + Earned Income + Net Income from Self-Employment + Interest Income + Dividend Income + Capital Gains Income + Tax-Free Interest Income + Pension Income + Distributions from an IRA or 401(k) = Modified Adjusted Gross Income.

Basically, MAGI is: ½ total household Social Security income + all other income. There are two kinds of income that are excluded from the formula: distributions from Roth IRAs and qualifying tax-free distributions from properly structured insurance products.

In 1983, if you were a single taxpayer, and your MAGI was in excess of $25,000, 50% of the excess amount over $25,000 was the amount of your Social Security that was taxable to a maximum of 50% of your total Social Security benefits.

If you were a married taxpayer filing a joint tax return in 1983, and your MAGI exceeded $32,000, 50% of the excess amount was the amount of your Social Security subject to income tax, once again to a maximum of 50% of your total Social Security benefits.

To make the point clearer, assume that a married couple, Victor and Beth, were both collecting Social Security benefits. Victor was collecting $21,000 per year, and Beth was collecting $19,000 per year.

In addition to Social Security benefits, Beth had a pension income of $12,000 annually, and Victor and Beth were taking combined IRA withdrawals of $14,000 per year.

Here is how their MAGI would be calculated:

½ Social Security ($40,000/2 = $20,000) + pension income ($12,000) + IRA distributions ($14,000) = Total Modified Adjusted Gross Income of $46,000.

Since the Social Security tax threshold in 1983 for a married couple was $32,000, Victor and Beth would take their total MAGI of $46,000 and subtract the $32,000 taxation threshold. That would leave $14,000.

$14,000 x 50% would mean that $7,000 of Victor and Beth's Social Security benefits would be taxable.

From 1983 to 1993, the Social Security tax thresholds for both single taxpayers and married taxpayers didn't change. Social Security benefits became taxable for single taxpayers at $25,000 of MAGI and at $32,000 for married taxpayers in every tax year from 1983 to 1993 with no indexing for inflation.

Then in 1993, another level of tax was added for Social Security benefits. The 50% tax level remained in place while an 85% level was added. The Omnibus Budget Reconciliation Act (OBRA) was passed in 1993. At the time, this change that made 85% of Social Security benefits taxable for some taxpayers was justified by proponents by saying the new tax would only apply to "higher income" beneficiaries.[12]

To be clear, OBRA didn't change these original Social Security taxation thresholds or raise them; OBRA just added another level of Social Security taxation.

After OBRA, a single taxpayer with MAGI exceeding $25,000 would still pay tax on their Social Security benefits to 50% of the excess. But if the single taxpayer's MAGI exceeded $34,000, 85% of the excess over $34,000 plus 50% of the difference between $25,000, and $32,000 was the amount of Social Security that would be subject to tax.

Put another way, after OBRA, single taxpayers would pay tax on Social Security benefits as follows: 85% of the excess over $34,000 of MAGI and 50% of the excess over $25,000 of MAGI would now be subject to income tax.

OBRA also added an 85% level of Social Security tax for married taxpayers. After OBRA, married taxpayers with MAGI exceeding $32,000 would still pay tax on their Social Security benefits to 50% of the excess. But if the married taxpayers' MAGI exceeded $44,000, 85% of the excess over $44,000 was the amount of Social Security that would be subject to tax.

Let's once again go back and look at the hypothetical example of Victor and Beth. As we noted above, Victor and Beth were both collecting Social Security benefits. Victor was collecting $21,000 per year, and Beth was collecting $19,000 per year.

Beth was also collecting pension income of $12,000 annually, and Victor and Beth were taking combined IRA withdrawals of $14,000 per year.

Here is how their MAGI would be calculated under the new, OBRA rules:

½ Social Security ($40,000/2 = $20,000) + pension income ($12,000) + IRA distributions ($14,000) = Total Modified Adjusted Gross Income of $46,000.

First, we calculate the level of Social Security benefits that would be taxed at 85%. The 85% threshold begins at $44,000 in MAGI. So, $46,000 – $44,000 = $2,000. $2,000 x 85% = $1,700.

Next, we calculate the level of Social Security benefits subject to the 50% rate. That would be 50% of the difference between $32,000 (the MAGI level where Social Security benefits are first taxed) and $44,000 (the MAGI level where 85% of Social Security benefits begin to be taxed):

$44,000 – $32,000 = $12,000 x 50% = $6,000.

Total Social Security benefits subject to income tax for Victor and Beth:

$6,000 + $1,700 = $7,700.

As you'll note, that's an increase of $700 in the amount of Social Security subject to tax from the 1983 rules.

Here is a very important point: these Social Security taxation levels have not changed since OBRA in 1993. Presently, a single taxpayer still pays tax on Social Security benefits with a Modified Adjusted Gross Income level of $25,000 or more. Married taxpayers still pay tax on Social Security benefits with a Modified Adjusted Gross Income level of $32,000 or more. This, despite the fact that the US dollar has lost a significant amount of purchasing power in that time frame.

So, as time has passed, and Social Security benefits have increased as a result of the annual cost-of-living adjustment, for many taxpayers the amount of Social Security subject to tax has increased each year.

Essentially, the taxation of Social Security benefits is just a method that the Washington politicians have adopted to cut the Social Security benefits of many Americans without their understanding that's actually what happened.

If you're a politician, and you cut Social Security benefits outright, everyone knows it. On the other hand, if you cut Social Security benefits by raising taxes via some obscure, hard-to-understand formula, it's far less obvious.

As time has passed, more and more Social Security recipients have seen their benefits cut as a result of this tax.

There may be a solution or a partial solution to this Social Security taxation problem for many Social Security recipients. More on that in Chapter Nine.

CHAPTER FIVE
More Social Security Collection Options and Strategies

There are many different collection strategies to consider and analyze prior to taking your Social Security benefits.

The collection strategies that may be available to you are dependent on your year of birth. Back in November of 2015, significant changes were made to Social Security collection methodologies.[13]

In this chapter, we'll discuss Social Security collection strategies in light of these new rules. As we discuss these collection options, certain strategies will apply only to some readers. When the November 2015 Social Security changes were made, certain collection methods were grandfathered for some Social Security beneficiaries.

When the Social Security rules changes of 2015, a collection strategy that allowed one spouse to file for Social Security benefits and then suspend those benefits while the other spouse collected a "spousal" benefit on those suspended benefits was eliminated.

There were also other changes to the way the spousal benefit would work moving forward.

To begin this discussion, we need to talk about spousal benefits and the deeming rules under Social Security.

To qualify for spousal benefits, you have to be at least 62 years old and married to your spouse for at least one year. Spousal benefits are half the spouse's Primary Insurance Amount when collecting at your Normal Retirement Age.

Typically, when one thinks about collecting spousal benefits, it's in terms of a lower earning spouse drawing benefits on the work record of the higher earning spouse.

Take the example of Paul and Hillary. Paul was the higher earner over the years and has a Primary Insurance Amount of $2,000 per month. Hillary can draw a spousal benefit of half of Paul's PIA once she reaches her Normal Retirement Age.

Assuming Hillary's retirement age is 66, she would be able to draw a spousal benefit of

$1,000 per month at that point.

Should Hillary elect to draw Social Security benefits at an age younger than her Normal Retirement Age, her benefit would be discounted. There is no financial incentive for Hillary to wait to collect spousal benefits at an age that is older than her Normal Retirement Age.

If Paul elected to collect Social Security benefits at an age younger than his Normal Retirement Age, say age 62, he would collect $1,500 per month, which is a 25% discount from his Primary Insurance Amount, but Hillary's spousal benefit is not affected. The spousal benefit is still based on Paul's Primary Insurance Amount of $2,000 monthly.

If Paul opts to collect Social Security benefits at age 62 and Hillary opts to collect at age 66, Paul's benefit will be $1,500 monthly while Hillary's benefit will be $1,000 per month.

One spouse can collect Social Security benefits based on the earnings record of the other spouse, but not vice versa. Spouses cannot elect to collect a spousal benefit on each other's work record at the same time.

The rules relating to spousal benefits under Social Security were modified with the law change mentioned earlier. This law change preserved a maximization strategy for some Social Security recipients and took it away for others.

If you were born before January 2, 1954, you have a maximization strategy available to you that those born after that date don't have. You can file what is known as a restricted application with Social Security.[14]

A restricted application simply means that when you apply for Social Security benefits, you are restricting your application to draw only spousal benefits.

In order to draw spousal benefits, your spouse needs to be collecting benefits. The exception to this rule is for those who are divorced. In the case of divorced spouses, if the couple was married for at least 10 years and have been divorced for two years or more, each ex-spouse can claim Social Security benefits on the other's earnings record, even if the ex-spouse had not yet claimed benefits. But the rule still applies, your birth date needs to be prior to January 2, 1954, in order to claim spousal benefits.

If you are eligible to draw spousal benefits, here's the maximization strategy to consider: draw spousal benefits at your Normal Retirement Age, and while you're drawing spousal benefits, your Primary Insurance Amount grows at the rate of 8% per year.

It's important to understand that assuming you qualify to file a restricted application for spousal benefits under Social Security, you must wait until your Normal Retirement Age to do so. If you apply to collect Social Security benefits at an age younger than your Normal Retirement Age, you are "deemed" to be applying to draw the highest benefit for which you are eligible.

Here's an example to make the point clear.

David turns 66 years old in 2019, which is the last year that those turning age 66 can consider this "restricted application" maximization strategy. His spouse, Sarah, is 69 and has been collecting Social Security benefits since she was 62 years of age.

David has the option to file a restricted application with Social Security and draw only spousal benefits on Sarah's work record, allowing him to collect half of Sarah's Primary Insurance Amount at his age 66. It's again important to note that David can draw half of Sarah's Primary Insurance Amount at his age 66 even though Sarah, by collecting her benefits at age 62, is drawing a discounted benefit.

David can now draw a spousal benefit for four years while his Primary Insurance Amount grows at a rate of 8% annually until he turns age 70. At that point, David can begin to draw his own benefit, which is his own Primary Insurance Amount times 132%.

If you were born prior to January 2, 1954, you have two options: one, you can file a restricted application under Social Security and draw only spousal benefits at you Normal Retirement Age (provided your spouse is collecting benefits), or, two, you can apply to collect Social Security benefits at an age that is younger than your Normal Retirement Age. If you decide to collect Social Security benefits prior to your Normal Retirement Age, you are deemed to be applying for the highest benefit for which you are eligible.

If you were born January 2, 1954, or after, you are deemed to be applying for the highest benefit for which you are eligible no matter how old you are the time you apply to collect benefits. In other words, if you were born January 2, 1954, or later, under the new rules, you cannot file a restricted application to draw Social Security benefits based upon your spouse's work record, which means you cannot use the restricted application maximization strategy.

If you were born prior to January 2, 1954, you can also draw a spousal benefit on an ex-spouse, provided you meet these criteria:

- You can't presently be married to someone else.

- You have to have been married to your ex-spouse for at least 10 years.

- You must be 62 years of age or older, and your ex-spouse must also be 62 or older.

- If you are younger than your Normal Retirement Age when you apply, you can't qualify for a larger benefit based on your own work record. In other words, if you are younger than Normal Retirement Age when you apply, the "deeming" rules apply. You will be deemed to be applying for the highest benefit for which you qualify.

If you meet all these criteria, the calculation for spousal benefits is just like the calculation for spousal benefits for married spouses, provided you and your ex-spouse have been divorced for at least two years. If you have been divorced at least two years, it is not necessary for your ex-spouse to be collecting Social Security benefits presently. However, if you've been divorced for less than two years, you ex-spouse must already be receiving Social Security benefits in order for you to collect spousal benefits.

Your former spouse won't ever find out that you're collecting benefits under his or her earnings record. Social Security can access your ex-spouse's records as long as you provide proof of marriage.

It also doesn't matter how many ex-spouses there might be who qualify for divorced benefits; it won't affect any other Social Security benefit recipient. There is no effect on any of the ex-spouses, the current spouse, or the worker. Every ex-spouse who qualifies could collect Social Security benefits on one worker's record.

If you were born January 2, 1954, or after, and elect to collect Social Security benefits at your Normal Retirement Age, you will get the higher of your own Primary Insurance Amount or 50% of your ex-spouse's Primary Insurance Amount because you will be "deemed" to be filing for the highest benefit for which you qualify.

If you were born January 2, 1954, or after, and claim prior to your Normal Retirement Age, your benefits will be reduced as we've already discussed.

And just like with spousal benefits, there is no benefit to defer or delay collecting Social Security benefits past your Normal Retirement Age.

If you were born prior to January 2, 1954, one strategy to consider is to draw the spousal benefit from an ex-spouse at your Normal Retirement Age, and draw your own benefit at age 70.

If you're drawing benefits on an ex-spouse's work record, those benefits stop if you remarry. But, after being married one year to your current spouse, you will be eligible for current spousal benefits. If you get divorced again, you may qualify for spousal benefits from either of your ex-spouses; you could even begin to collect benefits from your first spouse again.

Then, there is the topic of survivor benefits, often called widow or widower's benefits. These benefits are calculated using the deceased person's earning record. These are the qualifications to collect survivor benefits:

- Your deceased spouse must have been fully insured; in other words, he or she must have had their 40 credits.
- You must be at least age 60.
- The marriage must have lasted at least 9 months.
- You must not have remarried unless you did so at age 60 or older.

Calculating survivor benefits can be a little complicated. It depends on whether the deceased spouse took early benefits, waited to collect Social Security until he or she reached their Normal Retirement Age or delayed filing, as well as the age when the surviving spouse wants to begin collecting benefits. Depending on these facts and circumstances, the surviving spouse could get 100% of what the deceased spouse was already receiving or 82.5% of his or her Primary Insurance Amount if the surviving spouse has reached Normal Retirement Age. If the surviving spouse files prior to his or her Normal Retirement Age, he or she will receive less.

If the deceased spouse drew Social Security early, there is a chance that 82.5% of the deceased Primary Insurance Amount would be greater than 100% of the check the deceased was receiving at his or her passing. As long as the surviving spouse has attained Normal Retirement Age, Social Security will give the surviving spouse the larger of 100% of the deceased benefit at the time of death or 82.5% of the deceased Primary Insurance Amount.

If the deceased spouse had not yet begun to collect Social Security benefits and died prior to his or her Normal Retirement Age, the surviving spouse would collect 100% of the deceased Primary Insurance Amount. If the deceased had not yet begun to collect Social Security and died at an age that was later than his or her Normal Retirement Age, then the surviving spouse would receive 100% of the deceased Primary Insurance Amount plus any delayed benefit credits, again assuming the surviving spouse has reached his or her Normal Retirement Age.

Any time you decided to draw Social Security benefits at an age that is earlier than your Normal Retirement Age, your Social Security benefits will be reduced. A surviving spouse who elects to collect survivor benefits prior to attaining his or her Normal Retirement Age would have his or her Social Security survivor benefits reduced per the following chart.

Age at Which Survivor Benefits Are Collected	Age 66 Normal Retirement Age	Age 67 Normal Retirement Age
60	71.5%	71.5%
61	76.2%	75.6%
62	81%	79.6%
63	85.7%	83.7%
64	90.5%	87.8%
65	95.2%	91.9%
66	100%	95.9%
67		100%

In the event that the surviving spouse is still caring for a child of the deceased who is under age 16, the survivor benefit would be 75% of the Primary Insurance Amount, but only as long as the child is under the age of 16. When the youngest child being cared for reaches age 17, the survivor benefit stops until the surviving spouse turns 60 years old.

The most recent Social Security rule changes affected spousal benefits and divorced benefits, but survivor benefits did not change.

It's important to emphasize that when one spouse of a married couple passes away, there will be only one Social Security benefit paid to the survivor. That one benefit will be adjusted to the highest amount for which the survivor is eligible, but a survivor can't collect a survivor benefit and their own benefit. The survivor will collect the higher of the two Social Security benefits. If the survivor was receiving $1,500 monthly from Social Security and the deceased was receiving $2,000 monthly, the survivor would replace the $1,500 monthly benefit with the $2,000 monthly benefit. This is an important factor to consider when doing income planning.

If a widowed spouse remarries before he or she turns age 60, that spouse forfeits his or her rights to survivor benefits based on the deceased spouse's earnings record. If a widow or widower is contemplating remarriage and he or she is approaching age 60, it might be prudent to consider delaying that marriage until he or she turns 60. As already stated, if the new marriage happens after age 60, there is no change to the survivor benefits that a surviving spouse is collecting.

The best way to know the most favorable Social Security benefit collection option for you is to model all your options.

We have designed a process to do this using a Social Security maximization software program and a proprietary income-planning process. The reality is that with different collection rules applying to different beneficiaries, a comprehensive software program is the only way to accurately calculate Social Security benefit possibilities.

Once all the income options from Social Security are isolated, they should be plugged into an income-planning process that looks at total income desired during retirement and potential sources of income.

This process should not only look at Social Security maximization collection options but also survivor income options in the case of a married couple. The chapters that follow contain Social Security collection case studies to give you an idea as to how this process should work.

We offer a Social Security maximization evaluation as a service to introduce people to the kind of work our company does.

It's an easy process. You simply provide us with your Social Security earnings statement and answer a few questions. We never ask for personal information like Social Security numbers or account numbers, and you should never disclose those to anyone.

To order your Social Security
maximization analysis, simply visit
www.SocialSecurityMaximizationReport.com

CHAPTER SIX

Social Security Case Study: Considering All Personal Facts and Circumstances When Deciding When to Collect Social Security

In this chapter, we'll give you a maximization strategy that we've developed over time. We think it's the best method to use to determine when is the best time to collect your Social Security benefits.

As we've already discussed, unless you're disabled, the earliest age at which you can collect Social Security benefits is 62.

Should you elect to draw Social Security benefits at age 62, your benefit will be discounted. The amount of the discount will be dependent on when your Normal Retirement Age is.

If your Normal Retirement Age is 66, you can draw Social Security benefits at age 62, but your

Primary Insurance Amount will be discounted by 25%.

If your Normal Retirement Age is 67, you can draw Social Security benefits at age 62, but your Primary Insurance Amount will be discounted by 30%.

Also, as we previously discussed, if you were born from 1955 through 1959, your Normal Retirement Age increases by two months for each birth year that passes. For example, if you were born in 1955, your Normal Retirement Age is 66 years and 2 months, if you were born in 1956, your Normal Retirement Age is 66 years and 4 months, and so on.

If your birth year is 1955 through 1959, you can elect to collect Social Security benefits at age 62, and your Primary Insurance Amount will be discounted on a pro rata basis. The discount to the Primary Insurance Amount is increased by .83% to .84% per year. For example, if your birth year is 1955 and your Normal Retirement Age is 66 years and 2 months, the discount to your Primary Insurance Amount when collecting Social Security benefits at age 62 is 25.83%. These discounts increase for each birth year from 1955 through 1959.

When drawing Social Security benefits at an age younger than your Normal Retirement Age, you are deemed to be applying to collect the highest benefit for which you are eligible. This is true no matter your year of birth.

If you were born January 2, 1954, or after, you are deemed to be applying to draw the highest benefit for which you are eligible no matter when you decide to draw benefits. As we've already stated, if you were born prior to January 2, 1954, you still qualify to file a restricted application for Social Security benefits and apply only for spousal benefits.

It's also important to keep in mind that when collecting any benefit from Social Security at an age that is younger than your Normal Retirement Age, you are subject to the earnings limit of $17,040 annually as we discussed in a prior chapter.

So, the question we want to explore in this chapter is, when does it make sense to draw Social Security benefits at age 62?

We'll begin this discussion by looking at "break-even points." While the term "break-even point" is not an official Social Security term, it's a term that we all use in the context of determining when is the ideal time to collect Social Security benefits.

Let's assume that a worker has a Primary Insurance Amount of $2,000 monthly at age 66, which is also that worker's Normal Retirement Age. Should that worker elect to collect Social Security benefits at age 62, the Primary Insurance Amount will be discounted by 25% to $1,500 monthly or $18,000 per year.

Collecting $18,000 annually at age 62 through age 66 means that this worker has a "head start" of $72,000 by age 66 ($18,000 x 4 = $72,000).

However, by waiting to collect Social Security at age 66, the worker will collect $24,000 annually, which is an extra $6,000 per year ($24,000 – $18,000 = $6,000). To calculate the "break-even point," the head start of $72,000 is divided by the additional income received at age 66 of $6,000 per year, which results in a break-even point of 12 years.

At age 78, this worker will have collected the same amount of Social Security benefits starting at age 62 or age 66. Here's the math: $18,000 annually times 16 years is $288,000; $24,000 annually times 12 years is also $288,000.

It's important to note that this calculation assumes the constant purchasing power of the US dollar, which will not be the case. Central banks around the world have a stated objective to create inflation. Inflation is just a nice way of saying currency devaluation through an expansion of the money supply.

That said, we have to make the assumption that dollars collected from Social Security presently will be worth more than a dollar collected from Social Security in the future. What we don't know is what the future rate of devaluation will be. A good software program will allow you to change this assumption along with your Social Security collection options.

Going back to our age 78 "break-even" example, one would have to assume that the real break-even point in real dollar terms after adjusting for inflation would be later than age 78 since the dollars collected at age 62 are going to buy more than the dollars collected at age 78.

For many people, deciding when to collect Social Security is more than just calculating when the break-even point is. Other considerations are other sources of income, the income needed during retirement, survivor income needs, future mandatory distributions from retirement accounts, and taxation of present and future income.

Let's look at a hypothetical example.

Phil and Mary are both age 62. They were both born in 1957, and they are looking to retire at the present time. Phil has a stronger earnings history than Mary and has a Primary Insurance Amount of $2,100 monthly at his Normal Retirement Age of 66 years and 6 months as compared to Mary's Primary Insurance Amount of $1,400 monthly at the same Normal Retirement Age.

Phil and Mary would like to have $5,000 gross per month at retirement. Phil has $435,000 in his 401(k), and Mary has $234,000 in her 403(b) retirement plan at her nonprofit employer. Mary will also be entitled to a pension of $824 per month at her age 62 if she elects a her-life-only income option. If she wants the pension to continue for Phil at her death should she predecease him, the pension collected monthly falls to $687. They are not entitled to collect any other income during retirement and are not expecting to receive an inheritance that will significantly alter their net worth during their retirement years.

Should Phil and Mary decide to collect their Social Security benefits at age 62 when they retire, Phil would collect $16,508 per year while Mary would draw $10,890 annually. That would provide Phil and Mary annual income of $27,398 or $2,283 per month.

Mary is eligible for a pension of $687 per month at her age 62. When that is added to the $2,283 per month, Phil and Mary have a total income of $2,970 per month.

If Phil and Mary were to draw Social Security at age 62, they would need to take an income of $2,030 per month or $24,360 per year from their retirement accounts. The Chart 6.1 illustrates how this might affect their retirement accounts, assuming a 4% annual growth rate on their investments.

There are a couple of things to note from the chart. First, the growth assumption is quite conservative at 4%. Should the actual growth be higher or lower than 4%, the numbers illustrated could change significantly. Second, when Phil and Mary reach age 70½ and start taking required minimum distributions (RMD's) from their retirement accounts, the income that they're required to take in the form of required minimum distributions exceeds their income needs. They need to take $24,360 per year from their investments to reach their $5,000 per month income goal; however, at age 70 their required minimum distributions total $24,895. Over time, based on these assumptions, their combined required minimum distributions will exceed $42,000 per year.

Chart 6.1: IRA Analysis

Client Phil & Mary

Assumptions:

Assumed Growth Rate:	4%	Individuals Income Tax Brackets Return
Assumed Combined Tax Rate:	26.25%	to Current Levels in 2025
Current IRA Balance:	$669,000	
Client Age:	62	
Withdrawals: RMD's Only		

Year		Age	Balance	RMD Factor	Income Withdrawal (RMD Amount)	Estimated Taxes on All Income and RMD's	Cumulative Tax
1	2019	62	$669,000	0	$24,360	$6,395	$6,395
2	2020	63	$670,426	0	$24,360	$6,395	$12,789
3	2021	64	$671,908	0	$24,360	$6,395	$19,184
4	2022	65	$673,450	0	$24,360	$6,395	$25,578
5	2023	66	$675,054	0	$24,360	$6,395	$31,973
6	2024	67	$676,722	0	$24,360	$6,395	$38,367
7	2025	68	$678,456	0	$24,360	$6,395	$44,762
8	2026	69	$680,260	0	$24,360	$6,395	$51,156
9	2027	70	$682,136	27.4	$24,895	$7,282	$58,438
10	2028	71	$683,530	26.5	$25,794	$7,545	$65,983
11	2029	72	$684,046	25.6	$26,721	$7,816	$73,798
12	2030	73	$683,618	24.7	$27,677	$8,095	$81,894
13	2031	74	$682,179	23.8	$28,663	$8,384	$90,278
14	2032	75	$679,657	22.9	$29,679	$8,681	$98,959
15	2033	76	$675,977	22	$30,726	$8,987	$107,946
16	2034	77	$671,060	21.2	$31,654	$9,259	$117,205
17	2035	78	$664,983	20.3	$32,758	$9,582	$126,787
18	2036	79	$657,514	19.5	$33,719	$9,863	$136,649
19	2037	80	$648,747	18.7	$34,692	$10,148	$146,797
20	2038	81	$638,617	17.9	$35,677	$10,436	$157,232
21	2039	82	$627,058	17.1	$36,670	$10,726	$167,958
22	2040	83	$614,003	16.3	$37,669	$11,018	$178,977
23	2041	84	$599,388	15.5	$38,670	$11,311	$190,288
24	2042	85	$583,146	14.8	$39,402	$11,525	$201,813
25	2043	86	$565,494	14.1	$40,106	$11,731	$213,544
26	2044	87	$546,404	13.4	$40,776	$11,927	$225,471
27	2045	88	$525,852	12.7	$41,406	$12,111	$237,582
28	2046	89	$503,825	12	$41,985	$12,281	$249,863
29	2047	90	$480,313	11.4	$42,133	$12,324	$262,184
30	2048	91	$455,707	10.8	$42,195	$12,342	$274,528
31	2049	92	$430,053	10.2	$42,162	$12,332	$286,861
32	2050	93	$403,406	9.6	$42,021	$12,291	$299,152
33	2051	94	$375,840	9.1	$41,301	$12,081	$311,233

On a side note, that could create a taxable Social Security problem for Phil and Mary. At age 62, when Phil and Mary are taking income from their retirement accounts of $24,360 annually, $7,958 is the amount of their Social Security benefits subject to income tax under current tax law.

By age 85, when Phil and Mary are required to take a minimum distribution of $39,402 for the year, the level of their Social Security subject to income tax will be $20,743 under current law.

Also, by drawing Social Security benefits at age 62, the survivor benefit is $16,508 per year, which is the higher of the two Social Security benefits that Phil and Mary receive.

We would be remiss if we didn't also point out that these assumptions don't take into account a cost-of-living adjustment on Social Security.

Now let's consider what happens if Phil and Mary decide to retire at age 62 but not collect Social Security until age 66.

By waiting until age 66 to collect Social Security benefits, Phil's Social Security increases from $16,508 to $25,200. Mary's Social Security benefits increase from $10,890 to $16,800. That is a household increase in Social Security benefits received of $14,602 per year.

However, by delaying Social Security benefits until age 66, Phil and Mary will have to rely on their investments to a greater degree since the only income they will have will be from Mary's pension of $8,244 annually.

Since Phil and Mary want to have $5,000 monthly in gross income, that means they will need to pull $51,756 from their investments for four years until their Social Security begins at age 66.

But at that point, since their Social Security will be $42,000 annually rather than the $27,398 per year, they would only need to draw $9,756 from their investments. The next Chart 6.2 illustrates actual withdrawals after accounting once again for required minimum distributions.

One advantage of waiting until age 66 to draw Social Security benefits is that the survivor benefit increases from $16,508 to $25,200, providing more income replacement to a surviving spouse. The second possible advantage to deferring Social Security to age 66 is that the level of Social Security subject to income taxes might be lower over the longer term since the required minimum distributions are lower. There is also

Chart 6.2: IRA Analysis

Client Phil & Mary

Assumptions:

Assumed Growth Rate: 4%   Individuals Income Tax Brackets Return
Assumed Combined Tax Rate: 26.25%   to Current Levels in 2025
Current IRA Balance: $669,000
Client Age: 62
Withdrawals: RMD's Only

Year		Age	Balance	RMD Factor	Income Withdrawal (RMD Amount)	Estimated Taxes on All Income and RMD's	Cumulative Tax
1	2019	62	$669,000	$0	$51,756	$13,586	$13,586
2	2020	63	$641,934	$0	$51,756	$13,586	$27,172
3	2021	64	$613,785	$0	$51,756	$13,586	$40,758
4	2022	65	$584,510	$0	$51,756	$13,586	$54,344
5	2023	66	$554,064	$0	$9,756	$2,561	$56,905
6	2024	67	$566,081	$0	$9,756	$2,561	$59,466
7	2025	68	$578,577	$0	$9,756	$2,561	$62,072
8	2026	69	$591,574	$0	$9,756	$2,561	$64,588
9	2027	70	$605,091	$27	$22,084	$6,549	$71,047
10	2028	71	$606,328	$27	$22,880	$6,692	$77,740
11	2029	72	$606,785	$26	$23,703	$6,933	$84,673
12	2030	73	$606,406	$25	$24,551	$7,181	$91,854
13	2031	74	$605,129	$24	$25,426	$7,437	$99,291
14	2032	75	$602,892	$23	$26,327	$7,701	$106,991
15	2033	76	$599,627	$22	$27,256	$7,972	$114,964
16	2034	77	$595,267	$21	$28,079	$8,213	$123,177
17	2035	78	$589,875	$20	$29,058	$8,499	$131,676
18	2036	79	$583,250	$20	$29,910	$8,749	$140,425
19	2037	80	$575,474	$19	$30,774	$9,001	$149,426
20	2038	81	$566,488	$18	$31,647	$9,257	$158,683
21	2039	82	$556,234	$17	$32,528	$9,515	$167,198
22	2040	83	$544,654	$16	$33,414	$9,774	$177,971
23	2041	84	$531,689	$16	$34,303	$10,033	$188,005
24	2042	85	$517,282	$15	$34,951	$10,223	$198,228
25	2043	86	$501,624	$14	$35,576	$10,406	$208,634
26	2044	87	$484,689	$13	$36,171	$10,580	$219,214
27	2045	88	$466,549	$13	$36,729	$10,743	$229,957
28	2046	89	$446,919	$12	$37,243	$10,894	$240,851
29	2047	90	$426,063	$11	$37,374	$10,932	$251,783
30	2048	91	$404,237	$11	$37,429	$10,948	$262,731
31	2049	92	$381,480	$10	$37,400	$10,939	$273,670
32	2050	93	$357,843	$10	$37,275	$10,903	$284,574
33	2051	94	$333,390	$9	$36,636	$10,716	$295,290

Chart 6.3: IRA Analysis

Client Phil & Mary

Assumptions:

Assumed Growth Rate:	4%	Individuals Income Tax Brackets Return
Assumed Combined Tax Rate:	26.25%	to Current Levels in 2025
Current IRA Balance:	$669,000	
Client Age:	62	
Withdrawals: RMD's Only		

Year		Age	Balance	RMD Factor	Income Withdrawal (RMD Amount)	Estimated Taxes on All Income and RMD's	Cumulative Tax
1	2019	62	$669,000	$0	$51,756	$13,586	$13,586
2	2020	63	$641,934	$0	$51,756	$13,586	$27,172
3	2021	64	$613,785	$0	$51,756	$13,586	$40,758
4	2022	65	$584,510	$0	$51,756	$13,586	$54,344
5	2023	66	$554,064	$0	$51,756	$13,586	$67,930
6	2024	67	$522,401	$0	$51,756	$13,586	$81,516
7	2025	68	$489,470	$0	$51,756	$13,586	$95,102
8	2026	69	$455,223	$0	$51,756	$13,586	$108,688
9	2027	70	$419,606	$27	$15,314	$4,479	$113,167
10	2028	71	$420,463	$27	$15,867	$4,641	$117,808
11	2029	72	$420,780	$26	$16,437	$4,808	$122,616
12	2030	73	$420,517	$25	$17,025	$4,980	$127,595
13	2031	74	$419,632	$24	$17,632	$5,157	$132,753
14	2032	75	$418,081	$23	$18,257	$5,340	$138,093
15	2033	76	$415,817	$22	$18,901	$5,528	$143,621
16	2034	77	$412,793	$21	$19,471	$5,695	$149,317
17	2035	78	$409,054	$20	$20,150	$5,894	$155,211
18	2036	79	$404,460	$20	$20,742	$6,067	$161,278
19	2037	80	$399,067	$19	$21,340	$6,242	$167,520
20	2038	81	$392,836	$18	$21,946	$6,419	$173,939
21	2039	82	$385,725	$17	$22,557	$6,598	$180,537
22	2040	83	$377,695	$16	$23,171	$6,778	$187,314
23	2041	84	$368,704	$16	$23,787	$6,958	$194,272
24	2042	85	$358,714	$15	$24,237	$7,089	$201,362
25	2043	86	$347,855	$14	$24,671	$7,216	$208,578
26	2044	87	$336,112	$13	$25,083	$7,337	$215,915
27	2045	88	$323,470	$13	$25,470	$7,450	$223,365
28	2046	89	$309,920	$12	$25,827	$7,554	$230,919
29	2047	90	$295,457	$11	$25,917	$7,581	$238,500
30	2048	91	$280,321	$11	$25,956	$7,592	$246,092
31	2049	92	$264,540	$10	$25,935	$7,586	$253,678
32	2050	93	$248,149	$10	$25,849	$7,561	$261,239
33	2051	94	$231,192	$9	$25,406	$7,431	$268,670

the possible advantage of taking more money out of retirement accounts at a lower income tax rate due to the fact that personal income tax rates are now lower through the tax year 2025, reverting back to the old tax rates in 2026.

What if Phil and Mary decide to wait until age 70 to collect their Social Security benefits?

Phil's Social Security benefit will increase to $28,979 while Mary's will rise to $19,117 for a household total of $48,096. The obvious advantage here is that the survivor benefit will increase to $28,979.

And it will further reduce the required minimum distributions that will be required at age 70. The previous Chart 6.3 illustrates.

In our view, one of the best ways to determine when to collect Social Security benefits is to just put the required withdrawals from investments side by side in different collection scenarios, ignoring required minimum distributions. This scenario assumes that if required minimum distributions are taken, they are simply reinvested after taxes are paid on them.

This Chart 6.4 illustrates:

Chart 6.4: IRA Analysis

Client Phil & Mary

Assumptions:

Assumed Growth Rate:	4%	Individuals Income Tax Brackets Return
Assumed Combined Tax Rate:	26.25%	to Current Levels in 2025
Current IRA Balance:	$669,000	
Client Age:	62	
Withdrawals: RMD's Only		

Year	Age	Balance	SS Age 70 Income Withdrawal (RMD Amount)	Balance
1	2019	62	$669,000	$51,756	$669,000
2	2020	63	$641,934	$51,756	$641,934
3	2021	64	$613,785	$51,756	$613,785
4	2022	65	$584,510	$51,756	$584,510
5	2023	66	$554,064	$51,756	$554,064
6	2024	67	$522,401	$51,756	$566,081
7	2025	68	$489,470	$51,756	$578,577
8	2026	69	$455,223	$51,756	$591,574
9	2027	70	$419,606	$3,660	$605,091
10	2028	71	$423,853	$3,660	$619,148
11	2029	72	$446,080	$3,660	$633,768
12	2030	73	$460,117	$3,660	$648,973
13	2031	74	$474,715	$3,660	$664,785
14	2032	75	$489,898	$3,660	$661,231
15	2033	76	$505,687	$3,660	$598,334
16	2034	77	$522,108	$3,660	$716,121
17	2035	78	$539,186	$3,660	$734,619
18	2036	79	$556,947	$3,660	$753,858
19	2037	80	$575,419	$3,660	$773,866
20	2038	81	$594,629	$3,660	$794,674
21	2039	82	$614,608	$3,660	$816,315
22	2040	83	$635,386	$3,660	$636,821
23	2041	84	$656,995	$3,660	$862,228
24	2042	85	$679,468	$3,660	$886,571
25	2043	86	$702,840	$3,660	$991,887
26	2044	87	$727,148	$3,660	$938,217
27	2045	88	$752,427	$3,660	$965,599
28	2046	89	$778,718	$3,660	$994,077
29	2047	90	$806,060	$3,660	$1,023,694
30	2048	91	$834,496	$3,660	$1,054,495
31	2049	92	$864,070	$3,660	$4,086,529
32	2050	93	$894,826	$3,660	$119,844
33	2051	94	$926,813	$3,660	$1,154,491

Chart 6.4: IRA Analysis

SS age 66 Income Withdrawal (RMD Amount)	Balance	SS age 62 Income Withdrawal (RMD Amount)
$51,756	$669,000	$24,360
$51,756	$670,426	$24,360
$51,756	$671,908	$24,360
$51,756	$673,450	$24,360
$9,756	$675,054	$24,360
$9,756	$676,722	$24,360
$9,756	$678,456	$24,360
$9,756	$680,260	$24,360
$9,756	$682,136	$24,360
$9,756	$684,087	$24,360
$9,756	$686,116	$24,360
$9,756	$688,226	$24,360
$9,756	$690,421	$24,360
$9,756	$692,703	$24,360
$9,756	$695,077	$24,360
$9,756	$697,546	$24,360
$9,756	$700,113	$24,360
$9,756	$702,783	$24,360
$9,756	$705,560	$24,360
$9,756	$708,448	$24,360
$9,756	$511,452	$24,360
$9,756	$714,575	$24,360
$9,756	$717,826	$24,360
$9,756	$821,202	$24,360
$9,756	$724,716	$24,360
$9,756	$728,370	$24,360
$9,756	$732,171	$24,360
$9,756	$736,123	$24,360
$9,756	$740,234	$24,360
$9,756	$744,509	$24,360
$9,756	$748,955	$24,360
$9,756	$753,578	$24,360
$9,756	$758,387	$24,360

In this case, with Phil and Mary retiring at age 62, once all factors are considered, it seems to make sense for them to collect their Social Security benefits at age 66, relying on their investments for income from age 62 to 66.

To order your Social Security
maximization analysis, simply visit
www.SocialSecurityMaximizationReport.com

CHAPTER SEVEN
Maximizing Benefits If You Were Born Prior to January 2, 1954

If you were born prior to January 2, 1954, you have Social Security maximization strategies not available to those born on or after that date. You have the ability to file a restricted application for Social Security benefits, which means that you can restrict your application to drawing only spousal benefits.

If you were born January 2, 1954, or later, you do not have this option; but the information discussed in this chapter may still have some applicability to you.

The best way to demonstrate how a spousal benefit could be used when maximizing Social Security benefits is through a hypothetical example.

Let's take the case of Ben and Tamara. Ben is 66 years of age and was born prior to January 2, 1954, while Tamara is presently 62 years old.

Ben has been a higher earner over the years and has a Primary Insurance Amount of $2,600 monthly at his Normal Retirement Age of 66. Tamara's Primary Insurance Amount is $1,700 monthly when she reaches her Normal Retirement Age of 66 years and 6 months.

Ben is a business owner who loves what he does and has no plans to retire any time soon. Tamara is a retired educator who is receiving a pension since her retirement two years ago.

The question is, when should Ben and Tamara collect Social Security benefits.

There are several alternatives.

The first has Tamara waiting to draw benefits at her Normal Retirement Age and Ben drawing at his age 70.

The second option for Ben and Tamara has Ben drawing at his Normal Retirement Age of 66 and Tamara drawing a discounted benefit at age 62.

The third option has Tamara drawing Social Security benefits at her age 62 and Ben filing a restricted application for spousal benefits at his age 66 and then his full benefit with delayed benefit credits at his age 70.

A closer look at Ben and Tamara's personal financial situation finds that Tamara has a pension income of $31,000 annually and Ben has net business income of $120,000 per year. Since Ben has no immediate plans to retire, the couple is most interested in maximization strategies over the longer term.

Ben and Tamara have also built a nice-size nest egg. Tamara has a 403(b) plan with her former employer that has a balance of $323,000, and Ben has a SEP IRA of $657,000. When Ben decides to quit working in his business and retire, he will be able to sell his business. While there will be additional assets generated from the sale of the business, this eventual transaction won't have a significant bearing on how Ben and Tamara elect to draw Social Security.

Ultimately, Ben and Tamara would like to have at least $120,000 per year in gross income when Ben sells his business and retires. For planning purposes, we'll assume that happens at Ben's age 70, although Ben is not sure when that could occur.

So let's examine the collection options that Ben and Tamara have in light of their personal facts and circumstances.

First, let's examine option one. Tamara waits until her Normal Retirement Age of 66 years and 6 months to collect her Social Security benefits, and Ben waits until age 70 to collect his Social Security benefits.

Tamara will collect $1,700 monthly or $20,400 annually at her age 66 years and 6 months. Ben will collect $41,184 annually from Social Security at his age 70. The income plan developed to let Ben and Tamara determine the best way to collect their Social Security benefits is based on Ben's earliest retirement date of his age 70.

So Ben's Social Security benefit at his age 70 is $41,184 per year, and Tamara's Social Security benefit is $20,400 annually at her Normal Retirement Age of 66 years and 6 months. Tamara also receives a pension of $31,000 per year, which is paid to her on a joint and 100% survivor basis. That means that should Tamara predecease Ben, Ben will continue to receive the full $31,000 annual pension benefit. Those sources of income provide the couple annual income of $92,584 per year.

That means, to get to $120,000 gross income, Ben and Tamara will need to pull $27,416 from their investments each year.

Once again, it's essential to point out that Ben and Tamara will need to take more income than the $27,416 each year from their investments due to required minimum distributions, but we'll assume that any excess distribution over and above the $27,416 each year is taken and then subsequently reinvested.

While there are inherent flaws in any Social Security maximization analysis technique due to unknown variables like actual life span and law changes, this method is one that provides the best outcome in our view.

The Chart 7.1 illustration that follows illustrates this Social Security collection scenario.

Notice in this scenario that based on a 4% growth assumption, Ben and Tamara will easily be able to meet their objective of $120,000 gross annual income during retirement.

Another plus to this first option is that the survivor benefit is near the current Social Security maximum of $41,184 per year.

Should Tamara predecease Ben, Ben would keep his benefit of $41,184 annually and lose Tamara's benefit of $20,400 per year.

Chart 7.1: IRA Analysis

Client Ben and Tamara

Assumptions:	Ben's Account	Tamara's Account
Assumed Growth Rate:	4%	4%
Current IRA Balance:	$657,000	$323,000
Client Age:	62	62

Year		Ben's Age	Balance	Income Withdrawal
1	2019	66	$980,000	$0
2	2020	67	$1,019,200	$0
3	2021	68	$1,059,968	$0
4	2022	69	$1,102,367	$0
5	2023	70	$1,146,461	$27,416
6	2024	71	$1,163,807	$27,416
7	2025	72	$1,181,847	$27,416
8	2026	73	$1,200,608	$27,416
9	2027	74	$1,220,120	$27,416
10	2028	75	$1,240,412	$27,416
11	2029	76	$1,261,516	$27,416
12	2030	77	$1,283,464	$27,416
13	2031	78	$1,306,290	$27,416
14	2032	79	$1,333,029	$27,416
15	2033	80	$1,354,717	$27,416
16	2034	81	$1,380,393	$27,416
17	2035	82	$1,407,096	$27,416
18	2036	83	$1,434,867	$27,416
19	2037	84	$1,463,750	$27,416
20	2038	85	$1,493,787	$27,416
21	2039	86	$1,525,026	$27,416
22	2040	87	$1,557,514	$27,416
23	2041	88	$1,591,302	$27,416
24	2042	89	$1,626,441	$27,416
25	2043	90	$1,662,896	$27,416
26	2044	91	$1,700,993	$27,416
27	2045	92	$1,740,520	$27,416
28	2046	93	$1,781,629	$27,416
29	2047	94	$1,824,381	$27,416
30	2048	95	$1,868,844	$27,416
31	2049	96	$1,915,085	$27,416
32	2050	97	$1,963,175	$27,416
33	2051	98	$2,013,190	$27,416

One can see by looking at the chart, that Ben could replace Tamara's Social Security income from growth on their combined investment portfolios without touching principal if that is their objective.

As we already stated, Tamara's pension is paid on a joint and 100% survivor basis to allow Ben to keep the full pension in the event Tamara were to predecease him.

On the other hand, a far more likely outcome is Ben predeceasing Tamara. Tamara is younger than Ben, and women have a longer life expectancy than men.

Should Ben predecease Tamara as the probabilities prophesy, Tamara keeps Ben's $41,184 annual Social Security benefit and loses her benefit of $20,400 per year.

But how does this option compare with the other two options that Ben and Tamara have?

The second option that we are considering is Ben collecting his Social Security at his Normal Retirement Age, and Tamara collecting at her age 62.

Since Ben has no interest in selling his business and retiring and plans to continue to work and earn income, it makes no sense for him to

Chart 7.2: IRA Analysis

Client Ben and Tamara

Assumptions:		Ben's Account	Tamara's Account
	Assumed Growth Rate:	4%	4%
	Current IRA Balance:	$657,000	$323,000
	Client Age:	66	62

Year		Ben's Age	Balance	Income Withdrawal
1	2019	66	$1,011,200	$0
2	2020	67	$1,082,848	$0
3	2021	68	$1,157,362	$0
4	2022	69	$1,234,856	$0
5	2023	70	$1,284,251	$44,010
6	2024	71	$1,289,850	$44,010
7	2025	72	$1,295,674	$44,010
8	2026	73	$1,301,730	$44,010
9	2027	74	$1,308,029	$44,010
10	2028	75	$1,314,580	$44,010
11	2029	76	$1,321,393	$44,010
12	2030	77	$1,328,478	$44,010
13	2031	78	$1,335,847	$44,010
14	2032	79	$1,343,510	$44,010
15	2033	80	$1,351,480	$44,010
16	2034	81	$1,359,769	$44,010
17	2035	82	$1,368,390	$44,010
18	2036	83	$1,377,355	$44,010
19	2037	84	$1,386,679	$44,010
20	2038	85	$1,396,375	$44,010
21	2039	86	$1,406,460	$44,010
22	2040	87	$1,416,948	$44,010
23	2041	88	$1,427,855	$44,010
24	2042	89	$1,439,199	$44,010
25	2043	90	$1,450,997	$44,010
26	2044	91	$1,463,266	$44,010
27	2045	92	$1,476,026	$44,010
28	2046	93	$1,849,297	$44,010
29	2047	94	$1,503,099	$44,010
30	2048	95	$1,517,452	$44,010
31	2049	96	$1,532,380	$44,010
32	2050	97	$1,547,905	$44,010
33	2051	98	$1,564,050	$44,010

consider collecting Social Security benefits at an age younger than his Normal Retirement Age since he will forfeit Social Security benefits with income in excess of the Social Security earnings limit of $17,040 as we discussed in Chapter Three.

When considering the second option, to ensure an apples-to-apples comparison, since Ben isn't selling the business and retiring any time prior to age 70, we'll assume that he and Tamara will make the decision to invest his annual Social Security benefit from age 66 to age 70.

Then, as the Chart 7.2 illustrates, Ben and Tamara will require income from their investment portfolio of $44,010 per year in order to achieve their income goals of $120,000 gross annual income at Ben's age 70, which is his earliest retirement date.

As you can see from the chart, the first four years, when Ben is age 66 through age 70, their portfolio is growing at 4% plus Ben's annual Social Security benefit of $31,200.

To be clear, Ben would likely not be able to invest his unneeded Social Security benefits in his retirement account, but we are illustrating it that way on the chart for simplicity's sake. It would probably be more accurate to have a third investment column labeled "nonqualified" or non-IRA assets.

Regardless, this chart illustrates an approximate outcome and gives us an idea as to the best of the two Social Security collection options for Ben and Tamara.

A quick comparison of the two charts shows a break-even of about Ben's age 80 between the two collection strategies. Adjusting this break-even point for Tamara's age, the break-even is Tamara's age 76.

Assuming Tamara lives to age 90 and assuming a 4% growth rate, Ben and Tamara leave their heirs an investment portfolio inheritance of $1,824,381 using the first strategy versus $1,503,099 using the second strategy.

But there is a third collection option to consider.

Tamara decides to draw her Social Security benefits at her age 62. At that point in time, Ben has reached his Normal Retirement Age of 66. Because Tamara is collecting Social Security benefits when Ben reaches his Normal Retirement Age, Ben is eligible to collect spousal benefits that are half of what Tamara would collect at her Normal Retirement Age. Ben only has this collection option because he was born prior to January 2, 1954.

While Ben is collecting spousal benefits, his Primary Insurance Amount grows at 8% simple interest per year. This 8% growth annually occurs from age 66 to age 70, when it ceases.

In this case, since Tamara's Primary Insurance Amount is $1,700 monthly, Ben will receive half of that amount, or $850 monthly, if he files a restricted application for Social Security benefits at his Normal Retirement Age.

Ben collects spousal benefits from age 66 to 70 and then draws a benefit equal to 132% of his Primary Insurance Amount at his age 70, which is the latest date that delayed benefit credits are available. In this case, Ben draws $850 monthly or $10,200 annually until his age 70. Then, at age 70, Ben begins to draw $41,184 per year.

In order to allow Ben to draw spousal benefits, Tamara has to draw her Social Security benefits at age 62, which means her Primary Insurance Amount is discounted by 27.5%. That makes her age 62 benefit from Social Security $14,790 per year.

At age 70, which is Ben's earliest retirement date, their combined income prior to investment withdrawals will be as follows: Ben's Social Security is $41,184 per year, Tamara's Social Security is $14,790 per year, and Tamara's 100% joint and survivor pension is $31,000 per year, for a total of $86,974 per year.

That means that at Ben's age 70, the couple will need investment withdrawals of $33,026 annually to reach their desired, gross income level of $120,000 per year.

Assuming Ben draws spousal benefits, as we assumed in the prior collection methodology, he will invest them since he doesn't need them for income. The following Chart 7.3 illustrates.

Again, like in the prior examples, required minimum distributions from retirement accounts are not being illustrated. Any distribution in excess of the income that is required will be reinvested in these maximization analysis models.

And the reality is, that is often what happens in our experience. Since the required distribution is based on account balance and remaining life expectancy, as retirement account owners age, their required minimum distribution amount rises.

In this analysis model, the break-even point compared to the other two models is approximately Ben's age 80, which is Tamara's age 76.

Chart 7.3: IRA Analysis

Client Ben and Tamara

Assumptions:	Ben's Account	Tamara's Account
Assumed Growth Rate:	4%	4%
Current IRA Balance:	$657,000	$323,000
Client Age:	66	62

Year		Ben's Age	Balance	Income Withdrawal
1	2019	66	$990,220	$0
2	2020	67	$1,040,008	$0
3	2021	68	$1,091,808	$0
4	2022	69	$1,145,681	$0
5	2023	70	$191,508	$33,026
6	2024	71	$1,204,821	$33,026
7	2025	72	$1,218,667	$33,026
8	2026	73	$1,233,067	$33,026
9	2027	74	$1,248,042	$33,026
10	2028	75	$1,263,617	$33,026
11	2029	76	$1,279,518	$33,026
12	2030	77	$1,296,660	$33,026
13	2031	78	$1,314,179	$33,026
14	2032	79	$1,332,400	$33,026
15	2033	80	$1,351,748	$33,026
16	2034	81	$1,371,055	$33,026
17	2035	82	$1,391,551	$33,026
18	2036	83	$1,412,866	$33,026
19	2037	84	$1,435,033	$33,026
20	2038	85	$1,458,087	$33,026
21	2039	86	$1,482,064	$33,026
22	2040	87	$1,506,999	$33,026
23	2041	88	$1,532,932	$33,026
24	2042	89	$1,559,903	$33,026
25	2043	90	$1,587,952	$33,026
26	2044	91	$1,617,123	$33,026
27	2045	92	$1,647,461	$33,026
28	2046	93	$169,012	$33,026
29	2047	94	$1,711,825	$33,026
30	2048	95	$1,745,951	$33,026
31	2049	96	$1,781,442	$33,026
32	2050	97	$181,353	$33,026
33	2051	98	$1,856,740	$33,026

In this model, like the first model, the survivor benefit is Ben's fully maximized annual Social Security benefit of $41,184.

A side-by-side comparison has the first model slightly outperforming the third model.

Assuming a long life expectancy, Ben and Tamara are probably best off with Tamara drawing at her full retirement age and Ben drawing at age 70.

All maximization models need to be based on individual facts and circumstances.

The best Social Security collection model in this example could be a different one should Ben and Tamara have different objectives. Should Ben want to retire right away or Tamara desire to continue working, there may be a better way to have them collect Social Security.

To order your Social Security maximization analysis, simply visit
www.SocialSecurityMaximizationReport.com

CHAPTER EIGHT

Maximizing Social Security Benefits by Minimizing Social Security Benefit Taxes

One of the best, yet most often overlooked areas in which to maximize Social Security benefits is to minimize taxes on them.

For many Social Security beneficiaries, this means not only analyzing how to maximize Social Security benefits but also analyzing the best way to minimize income taxes over your lifetime.

In Chapter Four we discussed the Modified Adjusted Gross Income formula that is used to determine how much of one's Social Security benefits are taxable. To refresh your memory, it is:

½ Social Security Income + Earned Income + Net Income from Self-Employment + Interest Income + Dividend Income + Capital Gains Income + Tax-Free Interest Income + Pension

Income + Distributions from an IRA or 401(k) = Modified Adjusted Gross Income.

In our experience, the biggest reason Social Security benefits are taxable at an ever-increasing rate during retirement for many taxpayers is increasing required minimum distributions from a retirement account like an IRA, 401(k), or 403(b).

As time passes and a retirement account owner ages, the factor that is used to determine the amount of the required minimum distribution gets smaller; the factor is based on life expectancy.

To calculate the required minimum distribution (RMD), one takes the retirement account balance at the end of the prior year and divides by the RMD factor. Obviously, the smaller the factor, the larger the required minimum distribution is.

The fact that many aspiring retirees elect to save for retirement using tax-deferred retirement accounts like IRAs and 401(k)s means many of these retirees pay tax on an ever-increasing level of Social Security benefits as time passes.

In our view, much of what you've been told about IRAs and other retirement accounts is simply wrong.

Let's start with a very common bit of misinformation when it comes to IRAs, 401(k)s, or some other retirement account.

At some point, when deciding whether or not you wanted to use an IRA or 401(k) for your retirement savings, you were probably told that the tax deduction you get for contributing to an IRA, 401(k), or other retirement plan is good.

That's simply not true.

While tax deductions are good, tax deductions for contributions to a retirement account are not good because these tax deductions are not actually deductions—they're essentially loans made to you by the IRS.

The IRS will make sure this loan gets paid back when you retire plus massive amounts of interest; do not get fooled into thinking this loan is a real tax deduction.

A real tax deduction doesn't have to be paid back; there are no strings attached.

If you make a gift to charity, the amount of that gift is deductible on your taxes, and that's the end of the story. That's not true of a "deduction" taken for a contribution to an IRA or 401(k). When you deduct your contribution to an IRA or 401(k) on your tax return, there are plenty of strings attached.

89

When you take a tax deduction for a contribution to an IRA or 401(k), the IRS immediately places a lien on your retirement account. This lien is, in one sense, kind of like the lien the banker might place on your house when you take out a mortgage, in that the IRA or 401(k) account is collateral for the loan.

However, the difference between the loan the IRS makes to you and the mortgage loan you get from a banker is that the terms of the mortgage loan from the banker are defined in advance, outlined in your loan documents, and can't be changed.

That's not true of the loan the IRS makes to you when you take a tax deduction for a contribution to a retirement account. The terms of paying back that loan to the IRS are unknown and can be changed at any time by the IRS or the Washington politicians by simply changing the tax rules.

This lien that the IRS places on your account when you reduce the income reported on your income tax return by the amount of the contribution entitles the IRS to a portion of every withdrawal on that account for the rest of your life. Every time you take retirement income out of your retirement account for the rest of your life, the IRS requires you to make another payment to them.

The brutal truth is that the IRS, in exchange for giving you this loan, now becomes a joint investing partner with you in your retirement account.

The amount that you end up paying back to the IRS will increase as your account grows. So instead of paying back the principal plus interest to the IRS like you would on a mortgage loan, you forfeit a percentage of your account to the IRS for the rest of your life. When the IRA or 401(k) account is eventually passed to your heirs, the IRS, your investing partner in the account, will once again be there to take their share.

And here's the really alarming news: if tax rates rise, the amount that needs to be paid back to the IRS surges.

Think about that for a minute.

Would you take out a mortgage if the banker not only got principal and interest payments from you, but also got an ownership share in your house? And the banker could, at any time, change the terms of the loan?

You probably agree that someone would have to be crazy to enter into a loan agreement like that. But that's exactly what you're doing when you put money in an IRA or 401(k) and take an income tax deduction.

Let's look at an example.

A 30-year-old taxpayer in a combined tax bracket of 20% who contributes $5,000 per year to a retirement account for 10 years and then lets the account grow at a 5% annual growth rate to age 70, enjoys tax savings over the 10 years she contributes to the plan of $10,000. That $10,000 in income tax savings is a loan made to the taxpayer by the IRS.

The IRS is now a joint investing partner in the retirement account.

At retirement, assuming no change in tax rates and just a 4% growth rate on the retirement account, and assuming the taxpayer takes only required minimum distributions until age 90, the total taxes paid on the retirement account will be $101,562. Tax savings of $10,000— taxes paid of $101,562!

The original loan amount from the IRS was $10,000; total cost to pay back the loan is $101,562!

Good deal?

For the IRS, yes; for the taxpayer, not so much.

And we should point out once again, those numbers assume no change in tax rates. If future income tax rates were to increase, the cost to pay back this $10,000 loan could be higher. Should this taxpayer's combined tax rate increase to 30%, total taxes paid over her lifetime will be $150,842. That's a loan payback cost of $150,842 on a $10,000 loan.

Looking at these numbers, wouldn't it have made more sense to pay off the IRS when the contributions were made and keep all the growth for yourself rather than sharing it with the IRS?

But here's the potentially even worse news. Those calculations of taxes "saved" and subsequently paid don't include any allowance for the effect that required minimum distributions might have on the level of taxation of Social Security benefits.

That's why when figuring out the best way to maximize Social Security benefits, it also makes sense to look at methods and strategies that could be used to reduce the ultimate taxes paid on the Social Security benefits that will ultimately be collected.

Here's a hypothetical case study that does just that.

Take the example of Frank and Susan. They are both 60 years old and plan to retire at age 66.

They've already done some preliminary income planning and have determined from this planning that they will need $84,000 in annual income during retirement to meet their lifestyle needs and desires.

After conducting a Social Security maximization study like those outlined in this book, Frank and Susan have determined that they can receive $58,000 in total household Social Security benefits when they both reach age 70. To reach this level of benefits, Susan will draw her Primary Insurance Amount of $24,000 annually at her Normal Retirement Age, while Frank defers his benefit to age 70 and draws $34,000 per year.

During the first four years that Frank and Susan are retired, they will draw $60,000 per year from their investments; however, once Frank's Social Security benefits kick in, they will need to draw only $26,000 per year from their investments.

Based on conservative growth assumptions, Frank and Susan will have accumulated $1,200,000 in qualified retirement accounts like IRAs and 401(k)s by the time they retire.

A quick analysis finds that Frank and Susan will be required to take distributions in amounts greater than their income needs once they reach age 70½.

The Chart 8.1 illustrates.

While Frank and Susan will only need an income of $26,000 per year from their investment portfolio at age 70, because they will both be required to take distributions from their retirement accounts, they will be forced to withdraw $41,564 and claim that as income on their tax return.

Notice from the chart, which uses a conservative growth assumption of 4%, that by the time Frank and Susan reach 89 years of age, their RMD exceeds $70,000 per year.

If we examine how the age 70 RMD might affect Frank and Susan's tax return, we find that the RMD amount of $41,564 is reported as income on their tax return as an IRA withdrawal.

Frank and Susan are, at that point in time, collecting $58,000 in Social Security benefits, and after applying the Modified Adjusted Gross

Chart 8.1: IRA Analysis

Client Frank and Susan
Assumptions:

Assumed Growth Rate:	4%
Assumed Combined Tax Rate:	19.25%
Current IRA Balance:	$1,200,000
Client Age:	66
Withdrawals:	RMD's Only

Year		Age	Balance	RMD Factor	IRA Withdraw
1	2018	66	$1,200,000	0	$60,000
2	2019	67	$1,185,600	0	$60,000
3	2020	68	$1,170,624	0	$60,000
4	2021	69	$1,155,049	0	$60,000
5	2022	70	$1,138,851	27.4	$41,564
6	2023	71	$1,141,178	26.5	$43,063
7	2024	72	$1,142,040	25.6	$44,611
8	2025	73	$1,141,326	24.7	$46,208
9	2026	74	$1,138,923	23.8	$47,854
10	2027	75	$1,134,712	22.9	$49,551
11	2028	76	$1,128,568	22	$51,299
12	2029	77	$1,120,360	21.2	$52,847
13	2030	78	$1,110,213	20.3	$54,690
14	2031	79	$1,097,744	19.5	$56,295
15	2032	80	$1,083,107	18.7	$57,920
16	2033	81	$1,066,195	17.9	$59,564
17	2034	82	$1,046,896	17.1	$61,222
18	2035	83	$1,025,101	16.3	$62,890
19	2036	84	$1,000,700	15.5	$64,561
20	2037	85	$973,584	14.8	$65,783
21	2038	86	$944,113	14.1	$66,958
22	2039	87	$912,241	13.4	$68,078
23	2040	88	$877,930	12.7	$69,128
24	2041	89	$841,154	12	$70,096
25	2042	90	$801,900	11.4	$70,342
26	2043	91	$760,820	10.8	$70,446
27	2044	92	$717,989	10.2	$70,391
28	2045	93	$673,502	9.6	$70,156
29	2046	94	$627,479	9.1	$68,954
30	2047	95	$580,866	8.6	$67,543
31	2048	96	$533,857	8.1	$65,908
32	2049	97	$486,666	7.6	$64,038
33	2050	98	$439,537	7.1	$61,907
34	2051	99	$392,735	6.7	$58,617
35	2052	100	$347,483	6.3	$55,156

Income formula, $30,223 of those Social Security benefits are reported as taxable on Frank and Susan's tax return.

Under current tax law, a married couple is entitled to a standard deduction of $24,000. When applying that standard deduction amount against Modified Adjusted Gross Income, Frank and Susan are paying a total tax of $5,274.

But here's the point. As time passes and Frank and Susan are required to take larger RMDs from their retirement accounts, they are also required to pay income tax on a higher percentage of their Social Security benefits. Based on this 4% growth assumption, Frank and Susan pay income tax on a higher percentage of their Social Security benefits each year until they reach age 85, at which point their Social Security benefits are taxed at the maximum level.

The Chart 8.2 that follows shows total tax paid by Frank and Susan. It's important to understand that we are illustrating our estimates of the total tax that Frank and Susan will pay based on a 4% growth assumption and current tax law. We are also assuming a flat state income tax of 4.25%. Current individual income tax rates are set to revert to the personal income tax rates that were in effect in 2017 in the calendar year 2026, highlighted in yellow on the chart.

Chart 8.2: IRA Analysis

Client Frank and Susan

Assumptions:

		Assumed Growth Rate:	4%
		Assumed Combined Tax Rate:	19.25%
		Current IRA Balance:	$1,200,000
		Client Age:	66
		Withdrawals:	RMD's Only

Year		Age	Balance	RMD Factor	IRA Withdraw
1	2025	66	$1,200,000	0	$60,000
2	2026	67	$1,185,600	0	$60,000
3	2027	68	$1,170,624	0	$60,000
4	2028	69	$1,155,049	0	$60,000
5	2029	70	$1,138,851	27.4	$41,564
6	2030	71	$1,141,178	26.5	$43,063
7	2031	72	$1,142,040	25.6	$44,611
8	2032	73	$1,141,326	24.7	$46,208
9	2033	74	$1,138,923	23.8	$47,854
10	2034	75	$1,134,712	22.9	$49,551
11	2035	76	$1,128,568	22	$51,299
12	2036	77	$1,120,360	21.2	$52,847
13	2037	78	$1,110,213	20.3	$54,690
14	2038	79	$1,097,744	19.5	$56,295
15	2039	80	$1,083,107	18.7	$57,920
16	2040	81	$1,066,195	17.9	$59,564
17	2041	82	$1,046,896	17.1	$61,222
18	2042	83	$1,025,101	16.3	$62,890
19	2043	84	$1,000,700	15.5	$64,561
20	2044	85	$973,584	14.8	$65,783
21	2045	86	$944,113	14.1	$66,958
22	2046	87	$912,241	13.4	$68,078
23	2047	88	$877,930	12.7	$69,128
24	2048	89	$841,154	12	$70,096
25	2049	90	$801,900	11.4	$70,342
26	2050	91	$760,820	10.8	$70,446
27	2051	92	$717,989	10.2	$70,391
28	2052	93	$673,502	9.6	$70,156
29	2053	94	$627,479	9.1	$68,954
30	2054	95	$580,866	8.6	$67,543
31	2055	96	$533,857	8.1	$65,908
32	2056	97	$486,666	7.6	$64,038
33	2057	98	$439,537	7.1	$61,907
34	2058	99	$392,735	6.7	$58,617
35	2059	100	$347,483	6.3	$55,156

Chart 8.2: IRA Analysis

Est Fed Tax On WDRWL	Cumulative Tax	Net to Heirs	Net to Spouse	Taxable Income
$7,127	$7,127	$969,000	$1,200,000	$46,200
$7,942	$15,068	$957,372	$1,185,600	$46,200
$7,942	$23,010	$645,279	$1,170,624	$46,200
$7,942	$30,951	$932,702	$1,155,049	$46,200
$8,119	$39,070	$919,622	$1,138,854	$47,121
$8,569	$47,639	$921,502	$1,141,178	$49,895
$9,035	$5,674	$922,197	$1,142,040	$52,758
$9,515	$66,188	$921,621	$1,141,326	$55,712
$10,830	$77,019	$919,680	$1,138,923	$58,758
$11,434	$88,453	$916,280	$1,134,712	$61,897
$12,057	$100,510	$911,318	$1,128,568	$65,130
$12,608	$113,118	$904,691	$1,120,360	$67,995
$13,265	$126,383	$896,497	$110,213	$71,405
$14,029	$140,412	$886,428	$1,097,744	$74,373
$14,909	$155,320	$874,609	$1,083,107	$77,380
$15,798	$171,118	$860,952	$1,066,195	$80,421
$16,695	$187,814	$845,368	$1,046,896	$83,488
$17,598	$205,411	$827,769	$1,025,101	$8,657
$18,472	$223,883	$808,065	$1,000,700	$92,866
$18,829	$242,712	$786,169	$973,584	$94,087
$19,173	$261,885	$762,372	$944,113	$96,262
$19,500	$281,385	$736,635	$912,241	$98,333
$19,808	$301,193	$708,928	$877,930	$100,277
$20,091	$321,284	$679,232	$841,154	$102,067
$20,163	$341,447	$647,534	$801,900	$102,522
$20,193	$361,640	$614,362	$760,820	$102,715
$20,177	$381,817	$579,776	$717,989	$102,613
$20,108	$401,925	$543,853	$673,502	$102,179
$19,757	$421,682	$506,689	$627,479	$99,954
$19,344	$441,026	$469,050	$580,866	$97,343
$18,866	$449,891	$431,089	$533,857	$94,320
$18,318	$487,209	$392,983	$486,666	$90,854
$17,695	$495,905	$354,926	$439,537	$86,917
$16,733	$512,638	$317,134	$392,735	$80,831
$15,721	$528,358	$280,592	$347,483	$74,428
		Add'l Tax at Death:		**$66,890**
		Total Tax		**$595,249**

Should there be a slight variation in these assumptions, the illustrated outcome could be significantly different.

The chart shows that should Frank and Susan live to age 100, they will pay total taxes of $528,358 during their lifetime, and when their heirs inherit the retirement account balance of $347,483 at their death, there will be another $66,890 in taxes paid, assuming the heirs are in the same tax bracket as Frank and Susan.

Should the survivor between Frank and Susan pass away at age 90 rather than at age 100 as illustrated in the chart, total taxes paid will be $495,813 rather than $528,358.

While Frank and Susan have determined that for their personal financial facts and circumstances it's best for Susan to draw Social Security at her Normal Retirement Age and Frank to draw at his age 70, they haven't done any lifetime income tax minimization planning.

One reason for them to consider doing this type of planning is that individual income tax rates are lower presently and will revert to the prior income tax schedule in 2026. If it makes sense for them, they may be able to get money out of their IRAs now at a more tax-favorable rate and reduce their future required minimum distributions, which could also favorably impact the level of income taxes they may pay on their future Social Security benefits.

If you go back and review the Modified Adjusted Gross Income formula that is used to determine how much of one's Social Security benefits are taxable, you'll note there are two types of income that are not included in the formula: distributions from a Roth IRA retirement account[15] and distributions from a properly structured guaranteed insurance contract.

If you're not familiar with a Roth IRA, it's really the polar opposite of a traditional IRA. A contribution to a traditional IRA creates an immediate income tax deduction in the amount of the contribution. That contribution can be invested, and it will grow on a tax-deferred basis, but all distributions from that traditional IRA account are included on a tax return reported as income.

A Roth IRA is exactly the opposite. There is no income tax deduction on the contribution to a Roth. The contribution can be invested and grows on a tax-free basis, and withdrawals are also distributed income tax-free.

Presently, any traditional IRA account owner who desires can convert their traditional IRA account to a Roth IRA by simply paying taxes on the conversion amount. Once the income taxes on the conversion have been paid, the Roth account now grows income tax-free. A Roth IRA also has no requirement to take distributions at age 70½. Properly structured guaranteed insurance contracts basically work the same way.

Since Frank and Susan are six years away from retirement and since individual income tax rates are lower until 2026, might it make sense for Frank and Susan to consider "divorcing themselves from the IRS in their IRA" to potentially reduce the income taxes that they will pay over their lifetime?

Let's assume for discussion's sake that Frank and Susan have reported joint income each year from their employment of $150,000. Let's also assume that Frank and Susan elect to do Roth conversions or distributions to a properly structured guaranteed insurance contract on their entire retirement account balance over a five-year time frame.

The following Chart 8.3 illustrates what their income tax liability might look like.

Their present retirement account balance is $948,000. Based on a 4% growth assumption, they will have accumulated about $1,200,000 at their retirement age of 66, as we've already stated.

Chart 8.3: IRA Analysis

Client Frank and Susan

Assumptions:

Assumed Growth Rate:	4%
Current IRA Balance:	$948,378
Client Age:	60
Withdrawals:	RMD's Only

Year	Age	Balance	RMD Factor	IRA Withdraw	Est Fed Tax On WDRWL	Cumulative Tax
1	2019	60	$948,378	0	$173,957	$48,812	$48,812
2	2020	61	$805,398	0	$173,957	$48,812	$97,624
3	2021	62	$656,698	0	$173,957	$48,812	$146,436
4	2022	63	$502,051	0	$173,957	$48,812	$195,248
5	2023	64	$341,218	0	$173,957	$48,812	$244,060
6	2024	65	$173,951	0	$173,957	$48,812	$292,872
7	2025	66	$0	0	$0	$0	$292,872
8	2026	67	$0	0	$0	$0	$292,872
9	2027	68	$0	0	$0	$0	$292,872
10	2028	69	$0	0	$0	$0	$292,872
11	2029	70	$0	27.4	$0	$0	$292,872
12	2030	71	$0	26.5	$0	$0	$292,872
13	2031	72	$0	25.6	$0	$0	$292,872
14	2032	73	$0	24.7	$0	$0	$292,872
15	2033	74	$0	23.8	$0	$0	$292,872
16	2034	75	$0	22.9	$0	$0	$292,872
17	2035	76	$0	22	$0	$0	$292,872
18	2036	77	$0	21.2	$0	$0	$292,872
19	2037	78	$0	20.3	$0	$0	$292,872
20	2038	79	$0	19.5	$0	$0	$292,872
21	2039	80	$0	18.7	$0	$0	$292,872
22	2040	81	$0	17.9	$0	$0	$292,872
23	2041	82	$0	17.1	$0	$0	$292,872
24	2042	83	$0	16.3	$0	$0	$292,872
25	2043	84	$0	15.5	$0	$0	$292,872
26	2044	85	$0	14.8	$0	$0	$292,872
27	2045	86	$0	14.1	$0	$0	$292,872
28	2046	87	$0	13.4	$0	$0	$292,872
29	2047	88	$0	12.7	$0	$0	$292,872
30	2048	89	$0	12	$0	$0	$292,872
31	2049	90	$0	11.4	$0	$0	$292,872
32	2050	91	$0	10.8	$0	$0	$292,872
33	2051	92	$0	10.2	$0	$0	$292,872
34	2052	93	$0	9.6	$0	$0	$292,872
35	2053	94	$0	9.1	$0	$0	$292,872

Add'l Tax at Death:	**$0**
Total Tax:	**$292,872**

Should Frank and Susan elect to do Roth conversions or distributions from their retirement accounts to a properly structured guaranteed insurance contract, they may decide to spread the conversions or distributions over five years as the chart illustrates.

Note again, for consistency's sake, the taxes paid are our estimate of the total taxes that Frank and Susan might pay, including income taxes paid on income in addition to income taxes paid on Roth conversions or IRA distributions to a properly structured guaranteed insurance contract.

Total taxes paid in this scenario, using the same 4% conservative growth assumption, are $292,872 versus the total taxes paid of $595,249, assuming Frank and Susan do not pursue a plan to minimize income taxes over their lifetime.

That results in potential total tax savings of more than $300,000 in addition to the additional income Frank and Susan might receive by maximizing their Social Security benefits.

That's significant.

And the best part of this strategy is that 100% of Frank and Susan's income is tax-free for their entire retirement based on current tax law.

Should future income tax rates increase, Frank and Susan may be unaffected.

The bottom line is this: if you've accumulated money in a traditional retirement account like a traditional IRA or 401(k), the question is not "if" you will pay back the loan the IRS gave you when you made your contributions, the question is "when" you will choose to pay it back.

Examining a lifetime tax minimization plan when you do your Social Security maximization analysis is critical to maximizing your benefits over the long haul.

To order your Social Security maximization analysis, simply visit **www.SocialSecurityMaximizationReport.com**

CHAPTER NINE

Finding the Best Social Security Maximization Option for You

By now, you probably realize that determining the best way to collect your Social Security benefits can be complex and is more than a mathematical calculation as to when you "break even" by collecting at one age versus another age.

There are many different variables to consider and take into account, such as when you are planning on retiring, when your spouse is planning on retiring (if applicable), if you qualify to draw benefits on an ex-spouse or a deceased spouse, what other resources you have, the level of income you'd like to have during retirement, the importance of a survivor benefit, and the projected tax you may pay during your retirement years.

And this decision is arguably one of the most important if not the most important financial decisions that you will make in your entire life.

We'd like to offer you a word of advice based upon our experience working with hundreds of folks who were also facing this decision. Don't make a quick decision, and don't wait until the last minute to make a decision.

We've seen folks make the right decision, and we've also spoken to many at our events, workshops, and seminars who, now that they've been educated to a certain degree, realize that they made the wrong decision but it's now too late to change it.

It's smart to educate yourself and take advantage of every possible resource and perspective to ensure that you are making the right decision for you.

We'd like to help by offering you a Social Security maximization analysis. Just visit www. SocialSecurityMaximizationReport.com and complete the short questionnaire that you'll find there.

To receive your Social Security maximization analysis, you need only provide us with general information; we never ask for specific, personal information to prepare your report, nor should you ever provide that information to anyone.

When we receive your information, we will examine all variables and help you determine the best way for you to collect Social Security for your own, personal situation.

The nominal cost for the Social Security maximization analysis is just $49. The small fee helps us offset some of the cost of preparing an analysis that is so extensive and comprehensive.

You may be wondering why we would make such an offer.

The answer is simple.

We want to introduce you to the kind of work our company does. Our company, Retirement Lifestyle Advocates, helps people maximize their retirement and avoid financial mistakes. Some people who receive this analysis inquire about working with our company, and others don't.

Either way is OK with us.

Here is how the 4-step process works.

1. You provide some general information.
2. We may clarify some of this information if we have a question.
3. We prepare your written reports.
4. Your reports are delivered to you at no additional cost and no further obligation.

Should you have questions about your analysis once you receive it, we will be glad to answer them. We can answer questions via e-mail, or we can arrange for a phone conversation with one of our representatives.

You will also be entitled to ask to have different outcomes modeled for you until you're confident that you've received the report that works the best for you.

Best of all, your analysis comes with a 100% money-back guarantee. If, for any reason, you are dissatisfied with your analysis, simply return all the reports and income models to us, and we'll cheerfully provide you with a full refund with no questions asked.

To order your Social Security
maximization analysis, simply visit
www.SocialSecurityMaximizationReport.com.

FOOTNOTES

[1] Source: https://www.ssa.gov/history/briefhistory3.html

[2] Source: https://www.ssa.gov/planners/retire/background.html

[3] Source: https://web.stanford.edu/class/e297c/poverty_prejudice/soc_sec/hsocialsec.htm

[4] Source: https://files.taxfoundation.org/legacy/docs/soc_security_rates_1937-2009-20090504.pdf

[5] Source: https://www.ssa.gov/cola/

[6] Source: U.S. Budget, page 64, as reported by Forbes magazine, May 15, 2010

[7] Source: https://www.forbes.com/sites/merrillmatthews/2011/07/13/what-happened-to-the-2-6-trillion-social-security-trust-fund/#1b7834dc4947

[8] Source: https://www.ssa.gov/policy/trust-funds-summary.html

[9] Source: https://www.forbes.com/sites/merrillmatthews/2011/07/13/what-happened-to-the-2-6-trillion-social-security-trust-fund/#1b7834dc4947

[10] Source: https://www.marketwatch.com/story/10-things-social-security-wont-tell-you-1314999788631

[11] Source: https://www.ssa.gov/history/InternetMyths2.html

[12] Source: https://www.ssa.gov/history/InternetMyths2.html

[13] Source: https://www.thebalance.com/file-and-suspend-spouse-social-security-strategy-2388922

[14] Source: https://www.investmentnews.com/article/20170802/BLOG05/170809989/a-refresher-course-on-social-security-claiming-rules

[15] Source: https://www.forbes.com/sites/forbesfinancecouncil/2017/04/04/the-roth-ira-is-more-than-meets-the-eye/#7a5ae7771481

Made in the USA
Middletown, DE
21 May 2022

66005671R00066